AF269434

KENYA

BY A. W. BUCKEY

Essential Library

An Imprint of Abdo Publishing
abdobooks.com

ABDOBOOKS.COM

Published by Abdo Publishing, a division of ABDO, PO Box 398166, Minneapolis, Minnesota 55439. Copyright © 2023 by Abdo Consulting Group, Inc. International copyrights reserved in all countries. No part of this book may be reproduced in any form without written permission from the publisher. Essential Library™ is a trademark and logo of Abdo Publishing.

Printed in the United States of America, North Mankato, Minnesota.
102022
012023

Cover Photos: Karan Khalsa/Shutterstock Images (giraffes); Shutterstock Images (pattern)
Interior Photos: Shutterstock Images, 4–5, 9, 13, 25, 31, 42–43, 68, 70–71, 73, 83, 92, 101; Lifestyle Pictures/Alamy, 6; Elen Marlen/Shutterstock Images, 11; Fabian Gysel/iStockphoto, 14–15; Peter Hermes Furian/Shutterstock Images, 17 (Kenya); Web Tools/Shutterstock Images, 17 (globe); Eva Rijnkels/iStockphoto, 18; Ariadne Van Zandbergen/Alamy, 21; Bartosz Hadyniak/iStockphoto, 23; Tony Karumba/AFP/Getty Images, 24; Jeniffer Collee/iStockphoto, 26–27; iStockphoto, 29, 32, 36–37, 93; Cezary Wojtkowski/iStockphoto, 34; Luca Cavallini/iStockphoto, 38; James Wakibia/SOPA Images/Sipa USA/AP Images, 40; Lex van Lieshout/Pool/AP Photo, 41; Sebastian Castelier/Shutterstock Images, 45; Bettmann/Getty Images, 49; John Bulmer/Popperfoto/Getty Images, 51; Pedro Ugarte/AFP/Getty Images, 53; Simon Maina/AFP/Getty Images, 55; Authentic travel/Shutterstock Images, 56–57; Aleksandar Todorovic/Shutterstock Images, 60; Ivan Bruninho/Shutterstock Images, 61; Yasuyoshi Chiba/AFP/Getty Images, 63; Ramsey Cardy/Sportsfile/Getty Images, 65; Leonardo Cendamo/Hulton Archive/Getty Images, 67; Hamids Lens/iStockphoto, 72; Donwilson Odhiambo/SOPA Images/Light Rocket/Getty Images, 75; Tolga Akmen/WPA Pool/Getty Images News/Getty Images, 77; Ton Koene/VW Pics/AP Images, 80–81; Miaron Billy/Shutterstock Images, 85; Denys Kutsevalov/Shutterstock Images, 86–87; Dong Jianghui/Xinhua News Agency/Getty Images, 88; Brian Inganga/AP Images, 90–91; Juliya Shangarey/Shutterstock Images, 97; Paul Ellis/AFP/Getty Images, 98

Editor: Priscilla An
Series Designer: Maggie Villaume

Library of Congress Control Number: 2022940376

PUBLISHER'S CATALOGING-IN-PUBLICATION DATA

Names: Buckey, A. W., author.
Title: Kenya / by A. W. Buckey
Description: Minneapolis, Minnesota: Abdo Publishing, 2023 | Series: Essential Library of Countries | Includes online resources and index.
Identifiers: ISBN 9781532199462 (lib. bdg.) | ISBN 9781098274665 (ebook)
Subjects: LCSH: Kenya--Juvenile literature. | Africa--Juvenile literature. | Kenya--History--Juvenile literature. | Geography--Juvenile literature.
Classification: DDC 967.62--dc23

CONTENTS

CHAPTER ONE

A TOUR OF KENYA

Andrew was on the longest flight of his life—an overnight trip over the Atlantic Ocean, a quick stop in Germany, and another nine-hour flight southeast across Africa—but he was too excited to sleep. Now, he and his mom are finally at Jomo Kenyatta International Airport in Kenya's capital, Nairobi. He can't believe they really made it. When his phone turns on, he checks the local weather. It's warm and sunny today, and it will be warm and sunny tomorrow, just as he had hoped. While his mom checks the signs for baggage claim, Andrew sends a text to his best friend, Mutuma, who's back home in Washington, DC.

Nairobi is Kenya's capital city and is known as the Green City in the Sun.

The production team of the 2019 CGI animated film *The Lion King* had visited Kenya to research its landscape for the movie.

"Just landed in Nairobi. Did you ever find out what happened at the end of *The Lion King*?" It's an inside joke between the two of them. When Andrew was young, he went over to Mutuma's house to watch *The Lion King* on DVD. They were halfway through when Mutuma's dad, who was watching with them, got up and paused the DVD. He explained to the boys that many of the characters' names were from an African language called Swahili. Simba, he told them, was the Swahili word for "lion," and Rafiki the monkey's name meant "friend." Mutuma's dad said that he had seen warthogs like Pumbaa up close when he was a child growing up in a country called Kenya.

"Dad, I know all that!" Mutuma had said, trying to unpause the movie. "We want to keep watching!" But Andrew was fascinated. He wanted to know more about the language called Swahili and the place with lions and baboons in it. He went home that day and looked up Kenya on a map. He saw a country in East Africa next to the Indian Ocean, right where the equator circles the middle of the world. He read about the giraffes, leopards, and elephants that lived there, as well as the sea life along the coast. He learned about the history of Kenyan cities and the wealthy medieval kingdoms that welcomed ships from all around the world. He had dreamed of getting to see Kenya, and he was always jealous when Mutuma flew to Nairobi to visit his cousins in the summer. Now, it was finally his turn.

Andrew's mom is an environmental scientist who studies lake and ocean habitats. When Andrew heard about her work trip to Kenya, he got Mutuma to help him make a PowerPoint presentation about why he should get to come along. His mom finally agreed, and now he gets to spend his spring break seeing her work and spending a few days on a tour of the country.

Andrew looks out the window as the taxi drives them through Kenya's bustling capital. Nairobi reminds him a little of DC, with its skyscrapers and national museums. Their driver points out the Nairobi National Museum on their way into the city center. Andrew's mom wants to go back and visit later in their trip. But right now, they are both hungry. They head to a restaurant that Mutuma

recommended in Nairobi's city center. Andrew knows exactly what to order to fill them up—
nyama choma, grilled meat. They get huge portions of meat served with *kachumbari*, a chopped
vegetable salad, and *ugali*, a starch a little bit like
grits. They make balls of ugali with their fingers
and dip it into the juices of the meat for a rich,
filling, traditional meal. Andrew's mom doesn't
usually eat meat, but she can't resist the delicious
nyama choma.

"*Asante*," Andrew says to the waiter; he knows
it means "thank you" in Swahili. Andrew learned
some Swahili words and phrases from spending
time with Mutuma's family, and last year he started
studying the language on his own. He'd like to be
fluent in Swahili as well as English, as many Kenyans
are. English and Swahili are the country's two
official languages, and government documents,
newspapers, and TV stations use both. Many Kenyans also speak a third language.

The next morning, Andrew and his mom say goodbye to bustling Nairobi. They'll be back,
but it's time for Andrew's mom to visit Lake Turkana, which is in the north of the country and is
also called Lake Rudolf. They take a short flight on a small plane, and Andrew stares down at the

Nyama choma is typically grilled goat meat or beef.

vast, tree-lined savanna, hoping to see giraffes and elephants on the move. Lake Turkana is beautiful and quiet—not at all like busy Nairobi. It's like a giant oasis in a desert, more than 155 miles (250 km) long.[1] Flocks of flamingos, attracted by the lake's salty water, line the shores. Andrew and his mom get on a boat and travel out to Central Island, a collection of three active volcanoes that still release smoke. They will camp on the volcanic island tonight, near the water.

While Andrew's mom talks excitedly with her coworkers, Andrew has a conversation with the guide on their boat. This is a beautiful island, the guide tells him, but they should still be careful. There are more Nile crocodiles on Central Island than anywhere else in the world. When their boat docks, Andrew sees a crocodile lounging on the shore, staring lazily at them as if it's not hungry yet. That night at the campground, they eat tilapia, a kind of fish that also lives in the lake, and they watch out for the bats that make their home on the island.

The next day, while his mom is out getting water samples, Andrew reads up on their next destination: Mombasa. The ancient city is on a coral island in the Indian Ocean, and Andrew looks over Mutuma's recommendations for the best street food. Mombasa is a traditionally Muslim city, and its food reflects its history as a seaport, a place where many different cultures have intersected and blended. Mutuma's mom is from Mombasa, and she makes the best samosas he's ever had. He can't wait to try the spiced tea and mitai, a kind of coconut donut.

There are many local street markets in the bustling city of Mombasa.

After they leave Mombasa, Andrew and his mom will have three free days before they head back to Nairobi. They're going to travel south, to the area of the country where Maasai pastoralists live and work. There, they'll go on a safari by car, into the savannas where lions, gazelles, buffalo, and giraffes live by the baobab trees. This is the part of Kenya that first caught Andrew's imagination so many years ago. The Kenya he's seeing now, though, is so much more varied and interesting than he could ever have imagined.

A COUNTRY OF HARAMBEE

Kenya is a country with a long and rich history. Archaeologists have found some of the oldest evidence of human life on Earth in Kenya, and people may have lived there more than a million years ago. Today, Kenya is a diverse country of more than 50 million people from many different cultures and living many different lifestyles.[3]

Kenya's motto is *Harambee*, a Swahili word that means "pulling together." Today, Kenya pulls together cultural, economic, and geographical diversity into a complex national identity. It is a hub

ARCHAEOLOGY IN KENYA

Kenya is home to several archaeological sites, places where scientists dig for remains from the human and nonhuman past. Hyrax Hill has been excavated since the 1930s. There are remains of early human life there, such as burial grounds and games. At Gedi, a site on the coast, archaeologists have found the remains of a medieval Muslim city.

for international business, trade, and fashion, but it is also a place where people work to preserve traditional ways of life. Kenya is a place of great natural beauty and richness. Its land is very fertile, supporting a wide array of crops and animals. Kenya is world-famous for its beautiful savannas and fascinating wildlife, but its grasslands and rain forest are just some of its many rich and interconnected ecosystems.

However, Kenya has faced significant divisions as well as political, environmental, and cultural struggles. In past years, the country has had fierce, violent debates over how to structure its political system and how presidents should lead the country fairly. Young Kenyans face significant economic and environmental challenges, in the form of unemployment and poverty as well as threats to Kenya's resources. They are drawing on Kenya's history and spirit to face these challenges.

CHAPTER TWO

GEOGRAPHY

Kenya is located on the eastern coast of the African continent. Earth's equator runs through the center of the globe, dividing the world into northern and southern halves, called hemispheres. Most of Kenya sits above the equator in the Northern Hemisphere, but the country's largest cities are in the Southern Hemisphere. The country is about twice the size of the US state of Nevada. In 2022, Kenya was the 27th most populous country in the world and home to just less than 55 million people.[1]

Kenya borders Tanzania to the south. To the west, it borders Uganda and the shore of Lake Victoria. Lake Victoria, the largest lake in Africa, is shared by Tanzania, Uganda, and Kenya. Kenya borders South Sudan to the northwest and shares most of its northern border with Ethiopia. To the east, Kenya borders Somalia.

Kenya's scenic landscapes include the Masai Mara, a wildlife reserve in southwest Kenya.

The country also has 333 miles (536 km) of coastline along the Indian Ocean.[2] The Indian Ocean stretches from the southern tip of Africa to Australia and Asia.

Kenya is thus an East African country and an equatorial country, as well as part of what's known as the African Great Lakes region. Besides Lake Victoria, the other African Great Lake found in Kenya is Lake Turkana, to the north. Another major geographical feature that runs through Kenya is called the Great Rift Valley. In geological terms, a rift is a place where two or three tectonic plates pull away from each other.

Most of the African continent is located on one tectonic plate, called the Nubian plate. However, a smaller tectonic plate in East Africa, the Somalian plate, is pulling away from the Nubian plate and creating rifts. These rifts run from the Arabian Peninsula in western Asia to Mozambique in southern Africa. There are two geological rifts that run through Kenya: the western and eastern branches of the East African Rift System. These rifts tend to be sites of volcanic activity, where lava from underneath Earth's outer crust erupts to the surface. In fact, the country's highest mountain, Mount Kenya, is an inactive volcano created by the rift.

MOUNTAINS, HIGHLANDS, PLATEAUS, AND LAKES

Kenya is a geographically diverse country, with mountains, highlands, lowlands, and 64 lakes. The eastern part of the country is home to the lowlands, land close to sea level. The rifts in Kenya helped create its mountain ranges, including Mount Kenya. The central highlands reach their

MAP OF
KENYA

SOUTH SUDAN
TERRITORY DISPUTED BY SOUTH SUDAN, ETHIOPIA, AND KENYA
ETHIOPIA
Lake Turkana
UGANDA
SOMALIA
Lake Baringo
Meru
Kisumu
Nakuru
Mount Kenya
Tana River
Masai Mara National Reserve
Nairobi
Athi River
Tsavo East National Park
Lake Victoria
Tsavo West National Park
Galana River
LAMU ISLAND
TANZANIA
Tsavo River
Malindi
Mombasa
INDIAN OCEAN
N
E
S
W

KEY:
Capital
City
Point of Interest

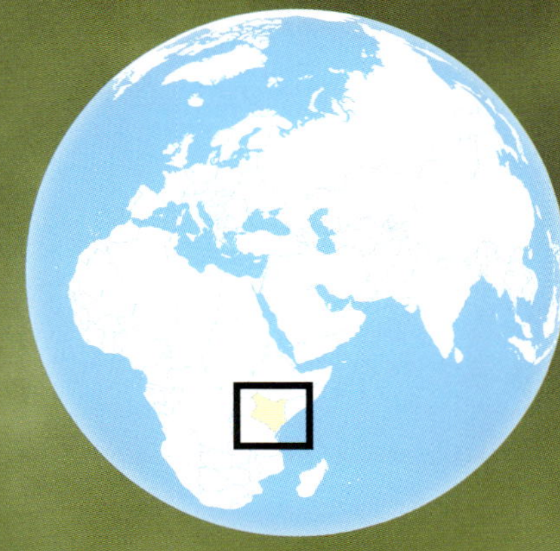

Mount Kenya National Park became a United Nations Educational, Scientific, and Cultural Organization (UNESCO) World Heritage site in 1997.

highest point at 17,057 feet (5,199 m) at the peak of Mount Kenya. In the western highlands, the highest elevation is 14,108 feet (4,300 m).[3]

However, not all of the land in the highlands is mountainous. Some of this higher-elevation land is in the form of plateaus, flatter stretches of land between mountain ranges. Northwest of Nairobi is Kenya's only rain forest, the Kakamega Forest. In the southwest of the country is the

Yatta Plateau, a large, hilly region created by the world's largest lava flow. Kenya's most humid climates and its most fertile soil are concentrated in the highland near Lake Victoria and on the southeastern coast of the country.

Northern Kenya is flatter and drier, with many wide plains. It is also where Lake Turkana, Kenya's second-largest lake, is located. Unlike Lake Victoria, Lake Turkana is a saltwater lake. It is nicknamed the Jade Sea because of its greenish color. There are a few mountainous areas in northern Kenya, such as the Matthews Mountain Range, which gets more rain than the rest of the country.

While Kenya has the least access to Lake Victoria of the three countries that share it, the lakeshore is an important hub of trade and economic activity. The major Kenyan city of Kisumu is located along the shore of Lake Victoria and connects to both lakeside trade and the Kenyan railway via the Kisumu railway station. Lake Victoria is also central to Kenya's fishing industry.

Southern Kenya, near the border with Tanzania, is occupied by hilly grasslands and savannas. These are important environments for pastoralists and animals such as wildebeests, antelope, and buffalo. The Kenyan coast is home to a wide variety of ecosystems, including mudflats, woodlands,

SHETANI LAVA FLOWS IN TSAVO WEST NATIONAL PARK

Tsavo West National Park is located in southeast Kenya, near the Indian Ocean Coast. Near the park, the Shetani Lava Flows serve as reminders of the power of tectonic rifts. Two hundred years ago, lava erupted from the earth in this spot, and the dried volcanic rock still looks like flowing liquid. These dangerous eruptions were named after *shetani*, the Swahili word for a devil spirit.

sand dunes, and mangroves, among many others. North of Mombasa is the Arabuko-Sokoke

Forest, the largest coastal forest in East Africa. This forest is a place of high biodiversity, meaning

it is home to a large variety of plant and animal

species. The Arabuko-Sokoke Forest is one of

several protected areas along Kenya's coast. It is

also a popular international tourist destination,

as visitors are attracted to its beautiful beaches,

wildlife, and coral reefs.

There are several islands off the coast of Kenya

that are part of the country's territory. Mombasa

Island is a part of the city of Mombasa and is

connected to the mainland by bridge. Lamu

Island is located about 150 miles (241 km) north of

Mombasa and is home to a town, also called Lamu,

as well as a port.[4]

KENYA'S CLIMATE

Kenya's climate varies according to elevation, season, and proximity to the nation's bodies of water.

In most places of Kenya, average temperatures are around 85 degrees Fahrenheit (29°C). The

coastal regions have average temperatures exceeding 80 degrees Fahrenheit (27°C).[5] These regions

Many people go to the Arabuko-Sokoke Forest for bird-watching. There are more than 230 bird species in the forest.

tend to experience high levels of humidity and rain compared to other areas. The weather near the great rifts tends to be cooler, with temperatures around 56 to 65 degrees Fahrenheit (13–18°C) in the southern part of the highlands.[6]

The seasons of the Northern Hemisphere and the Southern Hemisphere are the opposite of each other. While January is a winter month in the Northern Hemisphere, it is a summer month south of the equator. Kenya is located in both hemispheres, but the whole country follows a seasonal pattern closer to that of the Southern Hemisphere. Kenya typically experiences two rainy seasons. March to May is when the land receives heavier rainfall, while October to December is when there are only a few weeks of rainfall. Since the 1900s, global climate change has modified Kenya's climate and natural features. Between 2000 and 2020, the average temperature in the country increased by almost 0.92 degrees Fahrenheit (0.51°C).[7] Temperature increases can lead to heat waves, which may result in long periods of dry weather called droughts.

In Kenya, people, crops, and livestock depend on rainfall and groundwater. Droughts can lead to food shortages and famine. For example, in 2021, Kenyan president Uhuru Kenyatta declared a national state of emergency after droughts near Lake Turkana caused many livestock animals to die. By the end of 2021, 1.4 million food or dairy animals had died because of the drought. More than 3.5 million Kenyans faced food shortages.[9] The drought threatened to push Kenyans in the country's driest regions to famine, or the chronic lack of food.

People of the Maasai tribe need to walk long distances to get water because of persisting drought conditions.

In 2020, the lakes along the Great Rift Valley rose several meters, causing people to leave their homes. Scientists related the rising waters to climate change.

Global climate change can also cause sea levels to rise. This is because increasing temperatures melt polar ice, and warm water takes up more space than cold water. In Kenya, rising sea levels threaten coastal settlements, as well as the many ecosystems along the shore. When increased

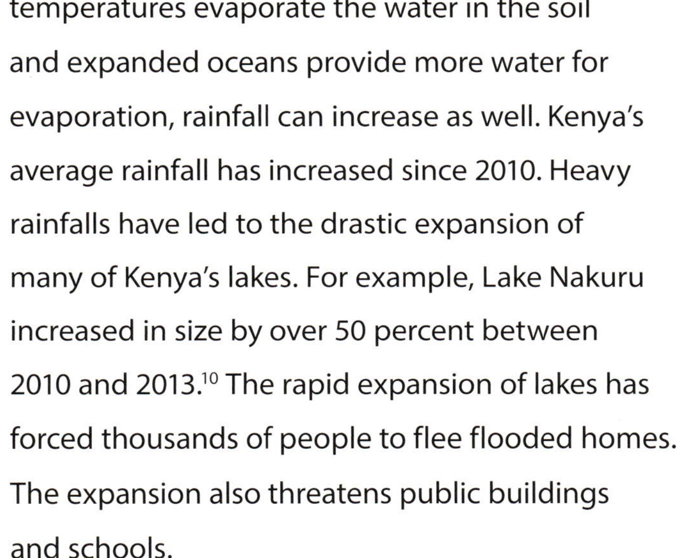

temperatures evaporate the water in the soil and expanded oceans provide more water for evaporation, rainfall can increase as well. Kenya's average rainfall has increased since 2010. Heavy rainfalls have led to the drastic expansion of many of Kenya's lakes. For example, Lake Nakuru increased in size by over 50 percent between 2010 and 2013.[10] The rapid expansion of lakes has forced thousands of people to flee flooded homes. The expansion also threatens public buildings and schools.

CHAPTER THREE

PLANTS AND ANIMALS

Kenya is home to some of the world's most famous wildlife. It is a popular destination for people to go on safari tours. The most popular safari location is Masai Mara National Reserve, which is on the savanna in southwest Kenya. A traveler on a Masai Mara safari would have a good chance of seeing many plants and animals that have fascinated humans for thousands of years.

Masai Mara National Reserve is named after the Maasai people, who have traditionally lived there. The word *mara* means "spotted," a reference to the occasional trees that spot the landscape. The most common tree found in the reserve is the acacia tree.

Cheetahs can be found in Masai Mara National Reserve. According to the IUCN Red List of Endangered Species, the cheetah population is listed as vulnerable.

Acacia trees are known for their fine, feathery leaves. The acacias of the Kenyan savanna are small- to medium-sized trees with wide, spreading branches. They provide shade for mammals and homes for birds, and they can also be used as firewood. The most common grass that grows in the savanna is called red oat grass, and it provides food for grazing animals such as zebras, ostriches, and gazelles that make their home in the reserve.

One of the most distinctive features of the reserve is the annual wildebeest migration that takes place from July through September. A wildebeest, also known as a gnu, is a large antelope with curved horns that can grow up to 31 inches (79 cm) long.[1] Wildebeests live in herds and travel around the plains of East Africa, following annual rain patterns in their search for food. Each year, more than a million wildebeests arrive at Masai Mara in search of the grasses that can sustain them through the dry season. Often, the zebras that live in the area join them in their travel. The journey is a dangerous one. They are vulnerable to attacks from predators such as crocodiles and big cats.

The savanna is home to prides, or groups, of lions. The lionesses live in these prides with their young, while adult males tend to wander alone. The lions of Masai Mara feed on prey as big as hippopotamuses, but they prefer prey such as wildebeests and will eat scavenged leftovers to save time. They share the land of the preserve with leopards, large spotted cats that hunt alone and like to stalk their prey from the park's trees. Cheetahs, the fastest land mammals on Earth, also live and hunt in the Kenyan savanna. Cheetahs can sprint short distances as fast as 68 miles per hour (110 kmh).[2] However, they get tired after their quick hunts and must rest before eating, so their prey can be snatched by the other scavengers of the park. These animals include the jackal,

The most popular wildebeest migration happens from July through September. However, wildebeests can migrate multiple times per year depending on rainfall.

an animal known for its nighttime singing and foul smell, and the vulture. The hyena, known for its laugh-like call, is famous for its love of carrion, or carcasses of already-killed animals. However, the hyenas of East Africa actually kill most of their food.

The other mammals of Masai Mara are no less impressive. The African savanna elephant is the world's largest land mammal, reaching a weight of nine short tons (8.2 metric tons).[3] The giraffe is the world's tallest land mammal and can grow up to 18 feet (5.5 m).[4] The Masai giraffe wanders the southern part of Kenya, while the reticulated giraffe can be found in the north and east. Around 400 Nubian giraffes, a critically endangered species, live in Kenya as well.[5]

Hippopotamuses populate the rivers and lakes of the reserve. They live in groups of cows, or female hippos, with one bull, or male, in each group. Lucky visitors to the savanna might get to see a black rhinoceros; there are about 600 in the country.[6] And Masai Mara is home to olive baboons, which wander in groups. The olive baboons hunt, forage for plants, and scavenge, always keeping an eye out for predators such as the big cats.

Many of these iconic Kenyan animals can also be found outside the boundaries of Masai Mara Reserve. For example, zebras and baboons both live near human settlements. Wild warthogs live throughout Kenya and have a reputation for destroying crops. Hippopotamuses and crocodiles use Lake Turkana in the north as a breeding ground. While the Kenyan savanna is an introduction to the great wildlife of the country, Kenya's biodiversity extends far beyond the grasslands and acacia trees.

WILDLIFE OF THE KENYAN COAST

There are coral reefs all along Kenya's shores. Coral is a small sea animal that secretes a substance called calcium carbonate. Over time, this substance becomes hard, like rock, and coral reefs are formed. The reefs provide shelter for fish and other sea animals, as well as places for seagrass to grow. There are more than 40 types of coral along the reefs of Kenya.[7] These coral reefs are filled with more than 350 fish species, many of which are brightly colored, such as parrotfish, wrasses, and

Kenya's reefs are among the largest in Africa, and they are part of the second-longest barrier reef in the world.

butterfly fish.[8] Several species of stingrays and sharks, which hunt in the shallow water, also roam the reefs.

Warm water temperatures can cause coral bleaching. This is when corals turn white because they lose important algae called zooxanthellae that are essential to their survival. Bleached coral is not dead, but it is weak and vulnerable. In 1998, Kenya's coral reefs had a devastating bleaching event, and the coral population has significantly decreased since then. When coral reefs weaken, the fish and wildlife that depend on the coral suffer. In turn, people who live on the coast and fish for a living are deeply affected. To combat the loss of coral reefs, Kenyan people are partnering with nonprofits to invest in the practice of coral gardening. In coral gardening, people grow coral species in nurseries and then plant the partly grown coral in wild reefs.

Many endangered species visit or live in Kenya's waters. There are five species of sea turtle that live in the Indian Ocean, and all of them are found in Kenyan territory. Humpback whales, dolphins, and manatee-like mammals called dugongs all swim in Kenyan seas. More than 11,000 species of marine animals populate Kenyan ocean waters.[9]

BIRDS OF KENYA

Kenya is home to more than 1,000 species of birds.[10] The largest bird is the ostrich. Two species of ostrich, the Somali ostrich and the Masai ostrich, live in the country. Ostriches can grow nine feet (2.7 m) tall.

Kenya has 68 Important Bird and Biodiversity Areas, which are designated to protect birds and wildlife.[11]

Flamingos flock in lakes like Lake Nakuru to feed on blue-green algae.

They are flightless and can escape predators by running up to 45 miles per hour (72.5 kmh).[12] In Kenya, ostriches are farmed for their meat, skin, and feathers.

The flamingos of Kenya live alongside beaches and lakes. They place their heads upside down in shallow water and eat small seeds, algae, and small marine animals such as mollusks. The reddish pigment inside the flamingo's food is what turns its feathers pink.

The African wood owl lives in the forests of Kenya. Also, a rare species called the Clarke's weaver, a yellow-bellied bird, is found only in Kenya. Other birds that make Kenya their home include egrets, eagles, hornbills, ducks, geese, and vultures.

KENYAN REPTILES, AMPHIBIANS, AND INSECTS

Kenya's most famous reptile is the Nile crocodile, but many other reptile species populate the country. The deadliest venomous snakes include the four species of cobra that live in the country and the puff adder. Puff adders enlarge themselves, or "puff up," before attacking, and their bites can be fatal to humans. The leopard tortoise, named for its spotted shell, lives in eastern Kenya, and the brown house snake and tropical house gecko are widely found in environments near where humans live. Luckily, neither is a threat to humans.

Several species of chameleon also live in Kenya. The chameleon is a lizard with a curling tail and a helmetlike shell called a casque on the front of its head. It has a unique ability to change its color to blend in with the environment. Jackson's chameleon is a species that lives in Tanzania and south-central Kenya. This chameleon is typically found in trees and gardens.

African chameleons catch insects with their sticky tongues.

Amphibians are animals such as frogs and toads that can live both in water and on land, although many live in just one or the other. In Kenya, bright-green and brown tree frogs can be found in the country's forests. Toads such as the desert toad, Egyptian toad, and Steindachner's toad can be found in dry areas like the savanna. One species, the Turkana toad, lives only on the shores of that lake. There is also a lesser-known type of amphibian found there, an animal called a caecilian. Caecilians live in wet dirt underground and look like worms.

Kenya's biodiversity extends to its insect population. There are more than 263 species of butterfly in the Arabuko-Sokoke reserve alone.[13] Also, about a quarter of Africa's dragonfly species are found in the country. While insects play a vital role in the ecosystems they inhabit, some can be dangerous to humans.

A mosquito's bite can be deadly. Female mosquitoes feed on the blood of mammals, such as humans, to nourish their eggs. In doing so, they can easily transmit diseases among humans and animals. One of the most common and dangerous mosquito-borne diseases in Kenya is malaria. Malaria invades and breaks human red blood cells and can cause severe illness and death. Seven out of ten Kenyans are vulnerable to malaria and must take preventive measures such as sleeping under mosquito nets, coverings that the insects cannot pass through.

The tsetse fly, a native African fly found in Kenya, is another bloodsucking insect. Both male and female flies attack humans and large animals to feed on their blood. The bite of the tsetse fly can transmit a parasite that causes a disease called African trypanosomiasis, or sleeping sickness. Sleeping sickness, as its name indicates, causes tiredness as well as fever and aches. While cases of sleeping sickness are much rarer than malaria cases in the country, rural Kenyans are still vulnerable to the disease.

DOMESTIC PLANTS AND ANIMALS IN KENYA

Agriculture, or the cultivation of plants and animals for human use, is an important part of the economy and people's livelihood. Kenya's main food crop is maize, or corn. Since the

Some dragonflies live only for a week, but others can live up to five years.

1920s, sugarcane has also been a major crop in the country.

Beef and dairy are very popular in Kenya, so domesticated cows make up a large proportion of Kenya's domesticated animals. While some cattle are raised on large-scale ranches, many domestic cattle are raised by pastoralists. Farming is one important source of fish in Kenya. The fish are kept in closed areas and harvested. Tilapia is the most commonly farmed fish in the country.

CONSERVATION EFFORTS IN KENYA

Kenyans and members of the international community are taking steps to protect Kenya's wildlife from harm. Kenya's wildlife is threatened not just by climate change but also by hunting, poaching, and habitat loss. In 2021, five Kenyan animal species were listed as critically endangered. These are the black rhino, the sable antelope, the roan antelope, an antelope called the hirola, and a primate called the Tana River mangabey.

The Kenya Wildlife Service is run by the government, and it cooperates with nonprofits and the European Union. The organization has set up wildlife sanctuaries and put measures in place to prosecute people who kill rare animals. However, these measures can be controversial.

The Kenyan government set a goal to plant 1.8 billion tree seedlings from 2018 to 2022.

Some poverty-stricken Kenyans poach, or illegally hunt, wildlife in order to survive. Others may kill animals such as elephants that threaten their crops.

Kenya has also become a leader in plant conservation. In Kenyan mountain regions, tree planting can improve watersheds, or areas that channel rain and snow into bodies of water. Trees help soil store water, preventing runoff of water to other areas. In this way, planting trees is a key tool for maintaining ecosystems and ensuring water access. Tree planting and harvesting can also be a sustainable source of income for Kenyan women in rural areas. The Green Belt Movement, started by environmentalist Wangari Maathai, is a Kenyan tree-planting initiative that began in 1977. Since then, the Green Belt Movement has helped plant more than 51 million trees in Kenya.[14]

WANGARI MAATHAI

Wangari Maathai was a scientist, veterinary specialist, and nonprofit founder. Maathai was born in rural Kenya in 1940 and pursued a scientific education, becoming the first Central and East African woman to earn a PhD. After finishing her studies, Maathai began working with the National Council of Women in Kenya. In 1977, she started an organization called the Green Belt Movement. Her local initiatives were led by women's groups and centered women's leadership in community development. Eventually, the Green Belt Movement planted millions of trees and expanded internationally. As Maathai's public profile grew, she used her platform to advocate for human rights and to speak out about public health issues such as the HIV/AIDS crisis.

In 2002, Maathai ran for National Assembly and was elected in a landslide, receiving 98 percent of the vote.[15] In 2004, she became the first African woman to win the Nobel Peace Prize. "More than simply protecting the existing environment," the Nobel Committee wrote, "her strategy is to secure and strengthen the very basis for ecologically sustainable development."[16] Maathai passed away on September 25, 2011.

Wangari Maathai was the first African woman to receive the Nobel Peace Prize and was the first female professor in Kenya.

HISTORY

In the distant past, there were several different species of hominids, or early humans. Neanderthals, for example, belonged to a now-extinct human species called *Homo neanderthalensis*. Some of these early human species, like *Homo rudolfensis*, lived in Kenya. Their bones have been found in archaeological sites in the country. Today, all human beings belong to the species *Homo sapiens*.

Scientists have found that all human beings are descended from a group of a few hundred people who lived in East and North Africa about 300,000 years ago. The first traces of these *Homo sapiens* in Kenya date back to 78,000 years ago. In 2021, archaeologists found the remains of a small child, buried with its body

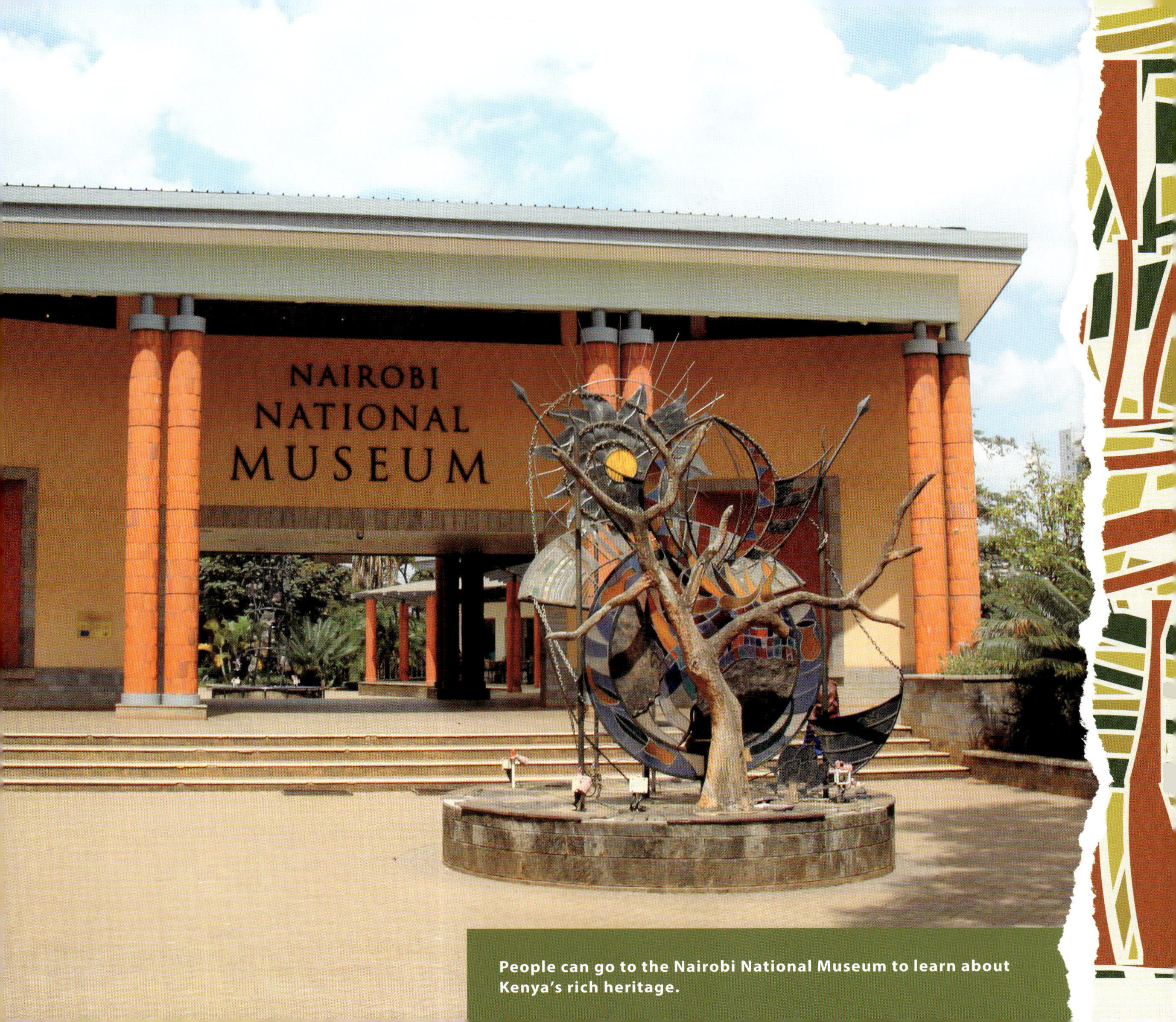

People can go to the Nairobi National Museum to learn about Kenya's rich heritage.

dressed and posed as if resting its head on a pillow. The child's remains are the earliest evidence of a very old human ritual: burying the dead. There are few other clues to what life was like in Kenya in the very distant past. However, the past several thousand years of Kenyan and human history are easier to trace. The languages spoken in the country give clues about what Kenyan cultures may have looked like thousands of years ago.

BANTU AND NORTH AFRICAN MIGRATIONS

The first people who lived in Kenya were hunter-gatherers. Between 3,000 and 5,000 years ago, people from what is now called Ethiopia moved southward and began living in what is now called Kenya. These people spoke Cushitic languages. Remnants of their culture, including shards of pottery, show that they lived in settled communities. A second wave of Cushitic speakers from present-day Ethiopia and Somalia followed. Nilotic languages, named after the Nile River, originated in East Africa. Around 2,000 years ago, Nilotic speakers from the north and west moved into what is now Kenyan territory. Some of these people lived around lakes and fished. While Kenya has undergone many historical changes since those migrations, the language families these migrants introduced have remained in the country.

Today, approximately 31 percent of Kenyans speak a Nilotic language, and about 4 percent speak a Cushitic language.[1] The Luo people, Kenya's second-largest ethnic group, speak a Nilotic language called Dholuo. Many of the nomadic pastoralist peoples of Kenya, such as the Maasai, also speak Nilotic languages. However, Kenya's most widely spoken language, Swahili, is a

Nearly all Kenyans living in the Lake Victoria region speak a Bantu language.

Bantu language. Today, there are more than 500 Bantu languages.[2] The history of Swahili dates to the Bantu migrations that began before 1000 BCE.

The Bantu migrations changed the cultural and demographic landscape of the African continent. The first people to speak Bantu languages lived in coastal West Africa, around modern-day Nigeria, Cameroon, and Gabon. These people were talented farmers who innovated a variety of techniques to make tools and weapons from iron. The Bantu peoples' iron-making knowledge gave them an advantage in farming and warfare. Eventually, the Bantu peoples began to move from their homeland into southern and eastern Africa. Historians suggest that their migration may have resulted from warfare, overpopulation, or epidemics. As they traveled, the Bantu peoples merged with local cultures and developed new groups and ways of life. This series of migrations took place over thousands of years. The Bantu peoples founded seaside towns and began to trade and farm. Over time, these East African settlements became powerful cities and towns with a unique multiethnic culture. This area was known as the Swahili Coast.

THE SWAHILI COAST

Muhammad, the prophet and founder of the Islamic faith, died in what is now Saudi Arabia in 632 CE. After his death, Arab Muslims rapidly expanded their territory across the Arabian Peninsula, Africa, and Asia. By the 700s CE, Islam had reached the coasts of East Africa. The people who lived in East Africa already had long-standing trade connections with Europe and Asia. The Muslim traders who came to live and work on the coast expanded these networks. Now, the coast was part of a larger Islamic world that included the Arabian Peninsula, Persia in modern-day Iran, and many places in East and Southeast Asia.

As trade flourished, so did the Swahili language and culture. Eventually, Kenya's port cities, like Mombasa, became important trade stops for sea travel between Africa and Asia. These cities were like small kingdoms with their own rulers. They even had diplomatic relationships with faraway kingdoms. For example, in 1414, the ruler of the city-state Malindi sent the Chinese emperor a giraffe. As these cities and towns developed their own language and way of life, Swahili culture was born.

Swahili is a Bantu language, but the word *Swahili* comes from the Arabic word for "coast." The language was influenced by the many cultures it was in close contact with. In addition, Swahili culture had customs of its own, like making buildings out of sea coral. While the largest Swahili settlements were on the coast, some people in inland Kenya were part of Swahili trading networks and had similar cultural practices.

In the 1490s, Portuguese traders arrived in Kenya for the first time. Eager to benefit from the region's trade networks, the Portuguese attacked Swahili city-states and set up their own settlements. The Portuguese succeeded in taking control of trade in the region. Portuguese missionaries also came to Kenya with the intention of converting the local population to Catholicism. The Swahili Coast had traditionally been a hub for the trade of enslaved peoples as well as goods. The Portuguese took over this slave trade but faced competition from the Dutch, who also wished to profit from African business networks and to enslave local people. For hundreds of years, the Portuguese and Dutch clashed with local powers for control over the region. For a time at the end of the 1600s, the Sultanate of Oman, a country in the southeast of the Arabian Peninsula, took control of Mombasa.

In the meantime, East African groups moved in and out of present-day Kenya, competing for territory and reorienting their lifestyles in the face of political change. For example, starting in the 1600s, the Kikuyu people moved into central Kenya from the northeast. The Maasai people, who live a traditional pastoralist lifestyle, arrived in their current homeland of southern Kenya around 1750. By the 1800s, however, a new power had emerged in the region—the British Empire, which by the early 1900s would be the largest and most powerful political body in the world. During the Berlin West Africa Conference of 1884–1885, major European powers gathered to discuss how they would divide power over land in central Africa. The United Kingdom obtained control over the land that is now Kenya.

BRITISH COLONIZATION OF KENYA

In 1895, what is now Kenya officially became part of the East Africa Protectorate. In 1920, the colony of Kenya was formed. British officials were

KIKUYU, KALENJIN, AND LUO

The Kikuyu, or Gikuyu, people are the largest ethnic group in Kenya. Kikuyu is a Bantu language. Traditionally, Kikuyu people farmed the fertile land in central Kenya. After the arrival of the British, the Kikuyu were the largest part of the colonial workforce. The Kalenjin people are members of several different Nilotic-speaking ethnic groups in Kenya and surrounding countries. The Luo people are native to western Kenya and speak a Nilotic language.

interested in Kenya's fertile land and resources. They wanted to enrich themselves, and they exploited native Kenyans in doing so. The United Kingdom seized large tracts of land from native Kenyans, sold it cheaply to British people to own and administer, and forced Kenyans to work the land as low-wage laborers. Coffee, tea, and sugarcane, all valuable commodities, were grown in the country.

During this time, Kenyan culture was strongly influenced by British colonists, and English became a language of politics and trade. While a few Kenyans cooperated with British officials in exchange for local power and influence, most Kenyans were opposed to British colonization. They suffered from widespread land theft and the many legal restrictions that kept them from exercising political and economic freedom.

Continued abuses by the British led to several organized rebellions against British rule.

British troops held Kenyan men at gunpoint while checking to see whether they participated in the Mau Mau uprising in the 1950s.

For example, the Mau Mau was a Kikuyu-led anti-imperialist movement that fought British rule in the 1950s. The British retaliated against the Mau Mau by using brute military force. Over the years of the uprising, about 11,000 Kenyans died in battle. The British placed about 20,000 Kenyan people into camps, where they were often tortured by officials and guards.[3] However, by the 1960s, the British Empire's power had significantly waned, and it began to withdraw from its former colonies. In 1963, Kenyans achieved independence from the British and established their own legislation. The Republic of Kenya was born.

DIFFICULT EARLY DECADES OF INDEPENDENCE

The first president of Kenya, Jomo Kenyatta, had been a Mau Mau fighter and was imprisoned by the British from 1953 to 1961. As president, Kenyatta repossessed land that the British had given to white farmers, and he redistributed it to native Kenyans. However, Kenyatta tended to favor

JOMO KENYATTA

Jomo Kenyatta, the first president of Kenya, influenced some of the most politically tumultuous eras in Kenya's history. Born Kamau wa Muigai in 1894, Kenyatta was fascinated by Western education. He received an English-language education, changing his name to Johnstone Kamau. He would later change his name to Jomo, meaning "burning spear" in the Kikuyu language, and Kenyatta, after a type of belt he enjoyed wearing.

Kenyatta was Kikuyu. In the 1920s, he became involved in the emerging movement demanding the return of colonized land to Kikuyu people. In the 1930s, Kenyatta was an official representative of Kikuyu interests. He spent much of the 1930s and 1940s in Europe, where he advocated for Kenyan rights. He returned to the country after the end of World War II (1939–1945). He married four times over the course of his life and had children with each of his wives. Uhuru Kenyatta is the second child of Kenyatta's fourth wife, the popular first lady Ngina Kenyatta.

Jomo Kenyatta was Kenya's president from 1964 to 1978.

members of his own ethnic group, the Kikuyu, when it came to handing out wealth and positions of power. Kenyatta permitted the existence of only his own political party, and he was widely suspected of having his rivals and enemies murdered.

In 1978, Kenyatta died and was succeeded by his vice president, Daniel arap Moi. Like Kenyatta, Moi favored his own ethnic group while in office, giving more government power and influence to Kalenjin people like him. Moi also banned political parties other than his own for almost a decade. After years of rule, Moi stepped down as president in 2002. In 2003, President Mwai Kibaki was elected. This was considered a significant moment in Kenyan politics, as Kibaki had run against Moi twice before and lost. However, after Kibaki narrowly won reelection in 2007 against Raila Odinga, a member of the Luo ethnic group, violence broke out in the country.

Ethnic tensions between the supporters of Kibaki and Odinga ran high. Some people protested Kibaki's win as a sign of continuing government corruption. The dispute over the elections led to riots in which more than 1,000 people lost their lives and many others were sexually assaulted.[5] In the aftermath of the violence, Kibaki retained his position as president. However, tension continued until February 2008, when an agreement was made to form a coalition government. A prime minister position was created, and Odinga was sworn into the post on April 17, 2008.

Many supporters celebrated when Mwai Kibaki was elected as Kenya's third president in 2002.

ELECTIONS AND CONSTITUTIONAL REFORM IN KENYA

In 2010, a majority of Kenyans voted to rewrite the country's constitution to solve years of political tension and corruption. The 2010 constitutional reforms removed the position of prime minister and limited the power of the president. According to the new constitution, the Kenyan Parliament has the power to approve or reject the president's decisions, such as cabinet appointments. In the past, the Republic of Kenya's government had unfairly redistributed land to favored people and groups. The new constitution created a land commission to review and address this unjust land distribution.

The new constitution also included a bill of rights, which laid the structure for cultural, economic, and cultural policies. The bill of rights included sections detailing freedom from discrimination, freedom of expression, and a right to fair and public hearings. It also established the Kenya National Commission on Human Rights.

In 2013, Uhuru Kenyatta, Jomo Kenyatta's son, was elected president of the country. In August 2017, President Kenyatta won reelection with 54 percent of the vote.[6] His rival was his former vice president and former prime minister Raila Odinga. Shortly after the results of the August 2017 elections, Odinga claimed that the results were manipulated and that he was the real winner. Kenya's Supreme Court declared the results of the election were "null and void." Although international observers had said they believed the election was fair, some observers claimed that Kenyatta and his supporters had adjusted the vote count.

The Supreme Court declared that a new election should take place within 60 days of the original one. However, Odinga decided to withdraw from this election and urged supporters to boycott the vote. As a result, Kenyatta won this second election with about 98 percent of the vote.[7] Kenyans from different political camps, as well as the international community, continue to disagree over the trustworthiness of the country's election process. However, the Supreme Court's

In November 2017, President Uhuru Kenyatta was inaugurated in Nairobi, Kenya.

decision was a display of the independence and power of judges in the country. Kenyatta's final term ended in August 2022. Kenyatta pledged to reduce corruption in the Kenyan political system and address income inequality.

PEOPLE AND CULTURE

Kenya is a multireligious, multilingual, and multiethnic country. According to one linguistic map, more than 70 languages are spoken in the country.[1] Kenya does not have a majority ethnic group; the largest group is the Kikuyu, who make up about 20 percent of the population.[2] The second-largest Kenyan ethnic group is the Luhya, who are about 14 percent of Kenyans.[3]

The Luhya group, like the Kalenjin, are made up of several smaller ethnic groups with some similar cultural roots and practices. The vast majority of Kenyans belong to native African ethnic groups. However, a small minority of Kenyans are South Asian. During the

Nairobi is an ethnically diverse city. Its major ethnic groups include Luo, Luhya, and Kamba.

British colonization of Kenya, the British Empire also ruled over modern-day Pakistan, India, and Bangladesh in South Asia.

When the British decided to construct a railway through Kenya, the Empire brought in South Asian people to work as low-wage laborers. These workers were not the first South Asians to live and work in Kenya. The region had been connected to the Swahili coast for centuries. However, it represented the first mass migration of South Asian people. These people and their descendants settled in Kenya, bringing their languages and cultures with them. According to the 2009 Kenyan census, about 46,000 Asian Kenyans are citizens in the country, with most living in Nairobi. White Kenyans, either descendants of white colonizers or people who moved more recently, had a slightly smaller population of 27,000. Together, these two populations make up about 0.1 percent of the country's total population.[4]

According to 2019 findings by the Pew Research Center, 93 percent of Kenyans say that religion is very important in their lives, and more than 70 percent believe that religion should be even more important in the country.[5] More than 85 percent of Kenyans are Christian, belonging to a wide variety of denominations, or branches of the faith with differences in belief and custom. Eleven percent of Kenyans are Muslim, and the rest belong to other religions or are nonreligious.[6] Christianity and Islam are not the only religions with a long history in the country. Many Kenyan ethnic groups have historically had their own religious beliefs. For example, the traditional Luo religion was monotheistic. The religion acknowledges just one god but discusses the existence of multiple spirits that can possess people and influence their behavior.

Today, some Kenyans blend Christian ideas with traditional beliefs from their ethnic groups. For example, in 1940, a Kenyan man named Elijah Masinde founded Dini ya Msambwa, a religion that incorporated some Christian stories and messages but emphasized resistance to European colonialism. Dini ya Msambwa also encouraged people to respect and continue practicing their ethnic traditions. Some Luhya people still practice Dini ya Msambwa. There are also some Kenyans who continue to practice their traditional beliefs.

The Maasai, or Maa-speaking people, are one of Kenya's most well-known ethnic groups despite being a minority in the country. One thing that sets the Maasai apart is their choice to live a traditional, low-tech lifestyle. The Maasai are nomads, or permanent travelers. They travel year-round, finding fresh pasture to feed their cow and goat herds. Maasai people dress in long cloths called *shuka* and tend to favor the color red. They also wear hand-beaded jewelry. Many Christian groups have tried to convert the Maasai people to Christianity. However, Maasai people continue to practice their traditional religion, worshipping a single god who manifests in different colors at different times.

The Maasai people live in southern Kenya and northern Tanzania.

Maasai people are both admired and criticized for their faithfulness to a traditional way of life. The shield on the Kenyan flag is meant to look like a Maasai shield, suggesting that Kenyans take pride in Maasai culture. However, the Maasai people face pressure to settle down and farm in smaller areas of land, even though they are nomadic. In addition, some criticize the cultural practices of Maasai people. For example, it's common for Maasai girls who reach puberty to be forced to marry older men, and few Maasai girls receive a secondary education.

KENYAN FOOD AND DRINK

Kenyan cuisine features the country's love of meat, especially beef, its enjoyment of spices, and the influences of the many global cultures it has interacted with. The most common starch, or carbohydrate, in Kenyan meals is ugali, a soft

Kenyans typically eat ugali with their fingers.

porridge made from maize. Ugali is a staple food that many Kenyans eat daily. People take a pinch in their fingers, roll it, and scoop meat, vegetables, and sauces into it.

The British introduced coffee and tea to Kenya, and both crops are still grown in the country. Kenya is the third-largest tea producer in the world, and tea is a common drink in Kenya. However, the tea Kenyans drink is closer to the Indian drink chai, which is spiced black tea mixed with hot milk. Often, chai is served with *mandazi*, a Kenyan donut-like puffy fried bread that can be spiced with cardamom. In fact, there is widespread Indian influence on Kenyan cuisine. Kenyans enjoy samosas, fried triangles of dough with spiced filling, and chapati, an Indian-style flatbread.

A lot of Kenyan small business owners sell unique foods and drinks, contributing to the country's street food culture. Kenyan street food is often cheap and widely available. Some urban Kenyans can afford to eat only once a day, so high-calorie, filling meals like meat soup are popular. *Dawa* stands, which are similar to smoothie stands, are another popular spot for street food. *Dawa* is the Swahili word for medicine, and it's common for Kenyans to make drinks called dawa for health benefits. Dawa stands have multiple recipes for these drinks, depending on the illness or desired effect. For example, one dawa maker named Peter Waichire swears by a drink made from mint, turmeric, sugarcane, lime, and ginger as a treatment for colds. Ginger, lemon, and honey tend to be core dawa ingredients, and garlic is also common. Like other Kenyan desserts and drinks, dawa often incorporates the sugarcane grown in the country. Dawa stands and vendors became even more popular during the COVID-19 pandemic, as many believed that drinking dawa could help ward off the disease.

Barbara Minishi, *left*, is a Kenyan fashion photographer and art director based in Nairobi.

One unique and classically Kenyan meal is made at a Nairobi restaurant called Golden Spot. The dish is made of extra-thin strips of beef marinated in lemon juice, tomato, onions, and ochuri, or cow bile. The restaurant named its classic dish the Anti-Theft as a joking reference to the cuts of beef that are so thin they can't be stolen.

FASHION IN KENYA

Kenyan fashion reflects the country's cultural, religious, and professional diversity. The high fashion industry is a presence in major cities such as Nairobi and Mombasa. The capital hosts multiple yearly fashion shows, highlighting the work of Kenyan and other East African designers. Contemporary Kenyan brands such as Bonkerz and Bongosawa blend streetwear with uniquely East African influences and materials. In Nairobi, award-winning jewelry-maker Ami Doshi Shah uses Kenyan materials to create cutting-edge designs that are featured in museums. One distinctive and versatile element of Kenyan fashion is the *kitenge*, a long, colorful cloth printed using a wax technique called batik. Kitenge typically come in bold, distinctive patterns and can be used as skirts, body coverings such as saris, or baby slings, among other uses.

Another element of Kenyan fashion and dress is the use of *mitumba*, a word that means "bundles" in Swahili. *Mitumba* refers to large shipments of used clothing donated to Kenya from other countries. When the clothing reaches Kenya, it is sold very cheaply in markets. Kenya is the largest importer of mitumba in East Africa. For some, wearing mitumba can be a necessity, but for others it is an opportunity to get a large wardrobe at a low price. However, native Kenyan designers and manufacturers argue that the flood of cheap clothes from the West makes it difficult for native businesses to succeed. In 2020, Kenya experimented with banning the import of mitumba. However, by 2022, the country had started to accept imports of mitumba again.

SPORTS IN KENYA

Kenyans are celebrated worldwide for their accomplishments in long-distance running. At the 2021 New York City Marathon, both the men's winner, Albert Korir, and the women's winner, Peres Jepchirchir, were Kenyans. The women's runner-up that year, Viola Cheptoo Lagat, was Kenyan

Eliud Kipchoge won the gold medal in the marathon at the 2020 Tokyo Olympics.

as well. This is not an unusual thing to happen in the long-distance running world. The New York City Marathon was held nine times from 2011 to 2021. Kenyan men won seven of those races, and Kenyan women won seven as well. In 2022, the current world-record holder in the men's marathon, Eliud Kipchoge, is Kenyan.

Many Kenyans also excel at running shorter distances. Between 1964 and 2021, Kenya accumulated 107 Olympic medals in track and field, which is 93 percent of Kenya's total Olympic medal count.[7] This might be because Kenya has an elite running culture, where promising runners can train together from a young age. Many Kenyans also live and run at high altitudes, where oxygen is less concentrated. In doing so, they train their bodies to process oxygen more efficiently, improving their performance. Unlike sports such as hockey or swimming, which require access to equipment and resources, running is a lower-cost sport to pursue. According a 2019 study from the Aspen Institute, track and field was the lowest-cost sport for children and teens to enroll in, making it a more accessible option for lower-income people. Kenya's reputation as a place to find new running talent means that international scouts and trainers look there for promising athletes to sponsor. Kenyans from low-income areas get the chance to become competitors.

Eliud Kipchoge broke a world record in 2019 when he ran a marathon and covered the 26.2 miles (42.2 km) in 1 hour, 59 minutes, and 40.2 seconds.[8]

KENYAN MEDIA, ENTERTAINMENT, AND STORYTELLING

Kenya's television and music culture form a vibrant part of the larger East African cultural world. The country has several TV stations, with some controlled by the government and some

Ngũgĩ wa Thiong'o is a celebrated Kenyan author. His first book is titled *Weep Not, Child*.

privately owned. The most popular, Citizen TV, is a private company. Some of Kenya's top TV shows include *Single Kiasi*, a show about single women in the city, and *Crime and Justice*, a show about police investigations. Kenya had more than 180 radio stations in 2021.[9] The country works hard to promote native Kenyan musical artists. In fact, Kenyan radio stations are required to play at least 40 percent Kenyan artists.[10] Popular Kenyan musicians include Afropop group Sauti Sol and pop singer Nameless. Kenya's film industry is small, but some Kenyan actors, such as Edi Gathegi and Lupita Nyong'o, have found international success.

Kenya has a thriving literary and storytelling tradition. One of the country's most famous authors is Ngũgĩ wa Thiong'o. Ngũgĩ was born in 1938, decades before Kenya became its own country. His first play, *The Black Hermit*, premiered in 1962 and celebrated the coming of Kenyan independence. Ngũgĩ became a professor in Nairobi in the 1960s. In 1972, he coauthored a famous paper called "On the Abolition of the English Department." The paper argued that Kenyans should study literature from an African point of view, rather than seeing literature as an extension of English language and culture. Ngũgĩ was successful in changing his department's name from English to Literature. Other Kenyan writers have also used literature as a way to discuss important issues in Kenyan cultures. For example, author Binyavanga Wainaina, who died in 2019 at age 48, wrote about his gay identity and advocated for gay rights in the country. He also satirized Western stereotypes about African people and stories. In a piece called "How to Write about Africa," Wainaina poked fun at clichéd descriptions of African landscapes. "The African sunset is a must," he wrote. "It is always big and red. There is always a big sky."[11]

KIKUYU PROVERBS AND RIDDLES

Kikuyu culture is well-known for its proverbs, riddles, and poetry. Proverbs are pieces of common wisdom, adapted to the vocabulary and expression of a particular culture. For example, one Kikuyu proverb says, "Having rain clouds is not the same thing as having rain." There is also a Kikuyu riddle that says: "I have a house without a door or a window." The answer? An egg.

CHAPTER SIX

POLITICS

Kenya is a presidential republic. This means that the people who lead the country and make laws are elected, rather than appointed, and that a president is the head of state. The United States is a presidential republic as well. Presidents in Kenya are elected for a five-year term and can serve another term if they are reelected.

Nairobi is Kenya's capital and the largest city in the country. It has a population of more than four million.[1] The next largest city, Mombasa, is much smaller, with a population of about 938,000 people.[2] The country is divided into 47 administrative sections. Today, Kenya's population is mainly clustered in the west of the country. The greater Nairobi area is densely populated, and so is the area near Lake Victoria. Other places with

Kenya's Parliament building is in the center of Nairobi.

high population density include Mombasa and the surrounding area on the southern coast, and Mandera, the Kenyan administrative district closest to Somalia.

Kenya's lawmaking body is called the Parliament. It is bicameral, with two different chambers. The Kenyan Senate has 68 seats, and the Kenyan National Assembly has 350. In each chamber, the majority of representatives are elected based on a simple majority vote. The Kenyan political system requires that at least 16 Senate members and 47 Assembly members be women. It also has two Senate seats and six Assembly seats representing the youth, and two Senate seats and six Assembly seats representing people with disabilities. The youth and disability representative Senate seats are elected, and the youth and disability representative Assembly seats are decided by Assembly members.

The Kenyan legal system incorporates influences from its multicultural history. Much of the Kenyan system is based on English ways of structuring and deciding court cases. The highest court in the country is the Supreme Court. It has seven justices who decide issues relating to presidential elections, as well as other matters of the Kenyan constitution. Kenya also has High Courts, which act as the final authority on civil and criminal cases. In addition, Muslim Kenyans can use the Islamic court system, or Kadhis' courts, for certain kinds of civil matters. In order to use the Kadhis' courts, every person involved in the case must be a Muslim who agrees to the court's legitimacy. For example, a married Muslim Kenyan couple who decide to divorce might use the Kadhis' courts to help them work out their case.

HISTORY OF THE KENYAN FLAG

The Kenyan flag was created in 1951, before Kenyan independence. The Kenya African Union, the most prominent political party at the time, wanted a symbol of African pride. The original flag had a spear in the center and black and red stripes. The spear honored both Kenyan traditional life and the importance of armed struggle. Today, the Kenyan flag has a black stripe for its people, a red stripe for human life, and a green stripe for land.

Kenya continues to adapt its legal traditions and customs to find a system that works best for its people. For example, there is a long-standing tradition in the United Kingdom that lawyers and judges should wear curled white horsehair wigs while in court. Until recently, Kenyan courts followed this tradition, and Kenyans also wore heavy robes in court. However, in 2020, the country's chief justice, Willy Mutunga, got rid of the wig-wearing custom and the tradition of calling judges "my lord" and "my lady." Instead, Mutunga said that lawyers and judges would be able to start wearing lighter robes more suited to Kenyan weather.

Kenyan courts intervened in 2022 when President Uhuru Kenyatta attempted a new set of reforms to the constitution. His reforms were called the Building Bridges Initiative, or BBI. Kenyatta tried to change the country's constitution so that the executive branch would have more power. For example, the BBI suggested that Kenya should have a prime minister appointed by the president. Many people in the country believed that this was Kenyatta's way of trying to find an important position for himself after his term as president ended. The reforms proposed by Kenyatta would also have cost the country a great deal of money.

In the end, Kenyan judges rejected Kenyatta's attempt to amend the constitution. "I endorse the findings of the two superior courts that the president ought not to be a player and an umpire in the amendment process," said the chief justice, Martha Koome, after the Supreme Court's decision.[4]

KENYAN POLITICAL PARTIES AND VOTING

During the rule of President Jomo Kenyatta, only one political party was permitted in the country. The Kenya African National Union, or KANU, was the ruling political body. Its time as the primary party in Kenya came to an end in 2002. After 2002, the number of political parties greatly increased. By 2022, the country had registered 85 parties. Some are large and influential, while others represent the interests of small ethnic or political minorities. In 2022, the right-wing

The former prime minister Raila Odinga created his own party called the Orange Democratic Movement (ODM) in 2005.

Jubilee Party, which is the party of the president, had the most representation in Parliament. The left-wing coalition, called the National Super Alliance, came in second.

Kenyans use biometric data, like fingerprinting, to ensure the identity of voters and the security of elections. Presidential candidates in Kenya must earn over 50 percent of the vote to be elected. In addition, they must receive at least a quarter of the votes in more than half of Kenya's 47 administrative districts. This rule is to help prevent the election of a candidate who is extremely popular in some areas of the country and extremely unpopular in others. If these conditions are not met in the first round of presidential elections, a second round of elections must be held.

KENYAN MILITARY AND INTERNATIONAL RELATIONS

Kenya spends about 1 percent of its gross domestic product (GDP) on the military, and military service is voluntary.[5] Its military faces pirates in Kenya's international waters and threats

Kenya and the United Kingdom maintain relations because of their shared history and interests. The UK prime minister Boris Johnson, *right*, met with Kenya's president, Uhuru Kenyatta, in January 2020.

from terrorist groups. One of the greatest security concerns is the Somalia-based terrorist group al-Shabaab.

Al-Shabaab's full name is Ḥarakat al-Shabāb al-Mujāhidīn, Arabic for Jihadi Youth Movement. The group emerged during a time of political strife in Somalia in 2006. It has survived as a terrorist and anti-government group. Its goal is to disrupt the Somali government, and it uses tactics such as civilian bombings to achieve its goals. Al-Shabaab opposes activities and organizations that it sees as threats to its concept of lawful Islamic government. Sometimes, its violence extends to Kenya, which lies to the south of Somalia. In 2013, the group carried out a terrorist attack in a mall in Nairobi. In 2015, it killed at least 147 college students in a Kenyan city called Garissa.[6] And in 2022, the group was suspected to have killed six Kenyans near the Somali border.[7] It's believed that these attacks were meant as revenge for Kenya's support of the Somali government.

Kenya and the United Kingdom have a complex ongoing relationship. Kenya is a popular tourist destination for British travelers. Partly as a result of the British presence in the country and partly because of the historical connection between the two nations, the United Kingdom and Kenya cooperate on military and counterterrorism matters. In 2021, Kenya signed the Defence Cooperation Agreement with the United Kingdom. As part of this agreement, the United Kingdom agreed to share counterterrorism information with the Kenyan government and to help train Kenyan soldiers.

The country also deals with maritime threats. International trade and travel, both legal and illegal, take place in the country's ocean waters. Sea trade makes up 90 percent of Kenya's regional trade, but people and ships in the Indian Ocean are vulnerable to terrorist threats as well as piracy.[8] In 2022, the Kenyan government announced that it had created a new committee to develop the country's National Maritime Security Strategy. One of the committee's first steps was to identify the biggest threats to Kenyan's oceans and to adopt standard international protocols for sea travel.

The borders between countries can be open or closed, heavily policed, or easy to cross freely. In central Africa, many people and groups do not fit neatly into the borders or identity of just one nation. For example, the Maasai people tend to travel between Tanzania and Kenya, following their herds. In northern Kenya, there are ethnic Somalis who share their culture with the people of Somalia. As a result, Kenya maintains varying levels of border control with its neighbors. For example, Kenya and Ethiopia have a porous border, which means it is easy to cross. This benefits people with cross-national businesses and families, but the border's porousness leads to some security concerns. For example, there is a thriving illegal drug trade that benefits from the lack of border control between the two countries.

Sometimes Kenya disagrees with its neighboring countries on how to handle border crossing issues. In 2017, the Kenyan government wrote a letter of protest to Tanzania after the Tanzanian government arrested Maasai herders who had crossed into Tanzania with their cattle. As the two countries disputed, it became clear that many people did not actually know where Tanzanian land ended and Kenyan land began. As a result, the two countries met in 2022 to begin clearly demarcating their border.

Kenya is an official member of the East African Community (EAC), an intergovernmental association that also includes Burundi, Rwanda, South Sudan, Uganda, and Tanzania. Culturally, Kenya belongs to the Swahili Coast, a region of coastal East Africa that extends from Mozambique to Somalia and shares a common Swahili history and culture.

CHAPTER SEVEN

ECONOMICS

The Kenyan economy had a GDP of almost 227 billion US dollars in 2020.[1] The country's GDP has seen an incredible increase since the 2000s as it focused on public and private sector investment, economic policies encouraging fiscal growth, and public infrastructure projects. The World Bank considers Kenya a lower-middle income country relative to the rest of the world.

The Kenyan shilling is the national currency. In the 2000s, the Kenyan government joined with other members of the EAC to create a joint currency similar to the euro. This money could be used in several East African countries. In 2019, however, the 2024 deadline to achieve this plan was delayed, and it became unclear whether this currency plan would come to pass.

Kenya is a leading exporter of black tea. The country also exports green and white teas.

Starting in the 2010s, the Kenyan economy began growing quickly, with an annual average growth rate of 5 to 6 percent.[2] However, as economic growth in Kenya increased, so did inflation. Inflation occurs when the prices of goods increase. So, for example, if a loaf of bread costs two dollars in 2020 but it becomes three dollars in 2022, inflation has occurred. When inflation happens rapidly, economic problems can arise. People may find that while the prices of basic goods and services have increased, their wages haven't. Global political events can cause inflation and deflation of the prices of international goods. For example, Ukraine and Russia supply Kenya with much of its wheat and cooking oil. The 2022 war in Ukraine disrupted supplies of these goods, leading to price inflation for wheat and cooking oil.

Different countries organize their economies in different ways. In a capitalist economy, the government does not play a large role in business. Instead, private individuals control trade. In a socialist country, the government takes control of many large businesses and industries, distributing their profits. The Kenyan government is a mixed economy, leaning in a

LIMESTONE

One of Kenya's largest natural resources is limestone, a versatile material with many different uses. Limestone is a major component of cement and is also a source of calcium carbonate used in common breakfast cereals and antacid tablets for stomach troubles. It's naturally formed from the interaction between sediment, or earth, and seawater. In Kenya, limestone is mined, or extracted from the ground, in the Rift Valley and Central regions. Other stones and minerals mined in Kenya include gold, iron ore, titanium, and gypsum ore.

capitalist direction. While private businesses have a lot of freedom and power, the government controls some key industries.

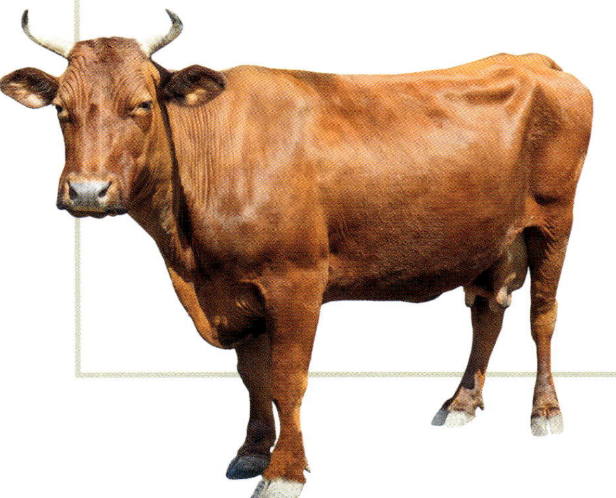

AGRICULTURE

The foundation of Kenya's economy is agriculture, which includes raising livestock and growing crops. About 60 percent of Kenya's workers are in farming, and the agricultural industry makes up about a third of the country's GDP.[3] Kenya's fertile land can grow a wide variety of crops, from potatoes to mangoes to sugarcane. The most popular Kenyan livestock industry is cattle farming. Cows are raised for both meat and dairy. Farmers also raise meat animals such as goats, camels, and pigs, poultry for meat and eggs, and donkeys and sheep for multiple uses.

Kenya is one of the leading exporters of cut flowers, or flowers grown for decoration, in the world. The country sells most of the flowers it grows to European markets. One of Kenya's most distinctive industries is its pyrethrum sector. Pyrethrum is a type of chrysanthemum flower that contains a toxin called a pyrethrin. These toxins are deadly to many insects such as mosquitoes without being toxic to humans. Pyrethrins are commonly used in pesticides, such as those used to protect crops. Kenya's conditions are ideal for pyrethrum growth, and in the 1980s, the country built the world's most efficient pyrethrum processing plants. However, in the 1990s, farmers lost pyrethrum profits because of corruption and government mismanagement, causing a steep decline in production. Since the 2010s, the Kenyan government has invested millions of dollars in trying to revive the pyrethrum industry. In 2017, it recruited more than 3,000 farmers to begin growing pyrethrum again.[4]

MANUFACTURING

Manufacturing is one of Kenya's largest industries. The country produces aluminum, steel, and lead, as well as plastics and textiles. Some of this manufacturing happens formally in factories and under the supervision of companies. However, there are also many Kenyans who work in microenterprises, or informal personal businesses. Microenterprise owners are often women. They make handmade goods or provide small-scale services without establishing official businesses. For example, many Kenyan women have found success starting small-scale businesses like food stands. Demand is high for microenterprise labor. In 2021, 90 percent of the demand for

Many Kenyans are successful in starting microenterprises. These can include local vegetable stands.

Many tourists visit Kenya for its national parks, where they can see a variety of animals.

new jobs came from microenterprises.[6] However, only about a third of microenterprise workers are full-time laborers.

TOURISM AND UNEMPLOYMENT

Tourism is another significant industry. The wildlife of the savanna and Kenya's beautiful landscapes are major attractions. Tourism-related businesses need hotel employees, restaurant managers, tour guides, wildlife management specialists, and activity guides such as scuba instructors. In the late 2010s, the Kenyan tourism industry employed about 9 percent of the country's workforce.[7] The COVID-19 pandemic paused tourism to Kenya for a time, and the industry suffered. Roughly 1.2 million Kenyans became unemployed because of the loss of international tourism.[8] The industry lost about 80 percent of its revenue before bouncing back in 2021, thanks in part to loosened travel restrictions.[9] Business owners and workers in the tourism sector were optimistic that the industry will continue to recover and regain its place in Kenya's economy.

Unemployment rates in Kenya are very high, as is poverty. It's estimated that as many as 40 percent of Kenyans cannot find jobs.[10] As a result, Kenyans who are able to leave the country to find employment

The Mombasa–Nairobi Standard Gauge Railway launched in 2017. Ridership and revenue in the first three months of 2022 were higher than the pre-pandemic levels of 2019.

often do so. These migrant workers send money home to relatives in the form of remittances. These remittances play an important role in the country's economy. In 2021, Kenya received more than $3.7 billion in remittance income.[11] More than half of remittances came from people living in North America. The handling and management of remittances is its own industry. Kenyans living abroad must find safe and reliable ways to ensure that the money they send home makes it into the right hands.

ECONOMIC DEVELOPMENT IN KENYA

Uhuru Kenyatta is committed to his predecessor's development plan, called Kenya Vision 2030. The goal of the plan is to lift Kenya from a lower-middle income country to a middle-income country through industrial and development projects. Since 2008, the plan has outlined multiple projects to modernize and improve all of Kenya's main industries. The expansion of fish farming is a part of Kenya Vision 2030. The country also welcomes foreign investors who can help the country reach its development goals. For example, one of Kenya's railways, a fast train line from Mombasa to Nairobi, was built by a Chinese company.

CHAPTER EIGHT

KENYA TODAY

Kenyans have a variety of lifestyles, and daily life is different for city dwellers, rural Kenyans, and pastoralists. About 30 percent of Kenyans live in cities, but it is difficult to generalize what their lives are like because income inequality is extremely high.[1] A 2018 study found that 20 percent of Nairobi residents controlled more than 86 percent of the city's wealth. In Mombasa, the top fifth of residents owned almost 80 percent of the city's wealth.[2] In the country at large, a small group of 8,300 people have more wealth than every other citizen of Kenya combined.[3] This means that cities have small pockets of extreme wealth, a large group of citizens living in poverty, and a moderately sized middle and upper class.

During the pandemic, the "coronavirus hairstyle" became a popular trend. It mimics the shape of the virus. This affordable hairstyle raised awareness about COVID-19.

Most of Kenya's richest citizens live in major cities where they can invest their wealth in high-value real estate. Kenya has one of the largest middle classes in Africa. The middle class consists of people who live between wealth and poverty. Middle-income Kenyans live in both rural and urban areas, working in professions or as successful farmers.

Overall, about 36 percent of Kenyans live in poverty.[4] In cities, Kenyans experiencing poverty tend to live in slums, informally constructed groups of houses on the outskirts of the city. People who live in slums often face poor sanitation and overcrowding that can lead to public health challenges. During the COVID-19 pandemic, people living in Kenya's slums were especially vulnerable to the economic and health toll of the pandemic. Lockdowns made people who sustained themselves and their families face unemployment or a drastic reduction in business. Additionally, because Kenyan hospitals charge for health care, many poor Kenyans couldn't access COVID-19 tests or ventilators. According to a Kenyan newspaper,

COVID-19 VACCINATION IN KENYA

In Kenya, rates of COVID-19 vaccination are extremely low. By November 2021, only about 9 percent of Kenyan adults were fully vaccinated against the disease.[5] At the end of 2021, the government announced a plan to require Kenyans to prove they were vaccinated before entering public buildings. But at the time, Kenya did not have enough vaccines in reserve to vaccinate the entire population. In December 2021, the country's High Court blocked the plan from going into effect.

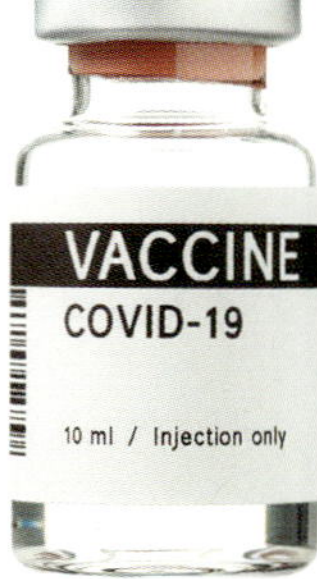

Kibera is a slum in Nairobi. It is the largest slum in Kenya by population.

one dark joke in Kenya's slums was that the pandemic was a "disease of the rich," because poor Kenyans have difficulty accessing health care.

People experiencing poverty in Kenya's rural areas face an overlapping set of challenges. With limited access to sanitation and health care, poor rural Kenyans are especially vulnerable to the effects of climate change. Recovery from unexpected damage to their crops, livestock, or living areas can be incredibly difficult.

VIOLENCE AGAINST WOMEN IN KENYAN SOCIETY

Kenyan runners can be heroes and role models for millions of their fellow citizens. The country was heartbroken when it lost one of those heroes, Olympic runner Agnes Jebet Tirop. The 25-year-old Tirop was a ten-kilometer runner and bronze medal Olympian who set a world record at an international race in September 2021. The next month, she was found stabbed to death in her home. The prime suspect was her husband, who had previously threatened to kill her. Tirop's murder put a spotlight on a widespread problem of violence and discrimination against women in Kenya. According to the Kenyan government, almost half of Kenyan girls and women experience intimate partner violence each year. According to a nonprofit called Human Rights Watch, rates of violence against women increased during the COVID-19 pandemic.

This epidemic of violence occurs in a context of discrimination against women in other areas of life. Women in Kenya are more likely to be poor than men, and many still undergo the banned practice of female genital mutilation. Activists for women's rights in Kenya hope that the widespread outrage and mourning over Tirop's death will help change attitudes about the seriousness of the problem in the country.

EDUCATIONAL CHALLENGES FOR YOUNG KENYANS

Kenya is a very young country. Forty percent of its population is 14 years old or younger.[7] Kenyan kids and teens grow up multilingual. At school, they learn in Swahili when they are young and English when they are older, and they often speak another language at home.

In Kenya, it's free to attend primary and secondary school. But there are financial barriers for participation in education. Kenyan children wear uniforms to school, but the cost of buying and maintaining them falls on individual families. This is a cost that can be difficult for many to manage. In 2021, the United Nations Children's Fund (UNICEF) estimated that more than a million Kenyan children who should be attending school are not doing so.[8] Some girls are forced to marry at a young age or drop out of school after becoming pregnant. About 18 percent of boys reported that they had to drop out of school to begin earning money for their families.[10]

ENVIRONMENTAL ACTIVISM AND LEADERSHIP IN KENYA

Kenya faces many internal challenges, but it is also helping lead the world in confronting the global challenges of climate change and environmental conservation. Wangari Maathai established a legacy of forward-thinking, creative environmental leadership that today's Kenyans are continuing to promote. For example, after growing up in Kenya's forests and watching them become sparser over time, young environmentalist Elizabeth Wathuti founded the Green Generation Initiative. Like the Green Belt Movement, the Green Generation Initiative sponsors tree planting, not just for local ecosystems but for the absorption of carbon emissions. Her organization also educates Kenyans and the world on environmental issues.

Kenyan students who want to move up to secondary school need to pass the national exam. Students receive the Kenyan Certificate of Primary Education if they pass the exam.

Young Kenyans, like environmental activist Rahmina Paulette, are hopeful for a better Kenya.

"This is humanity's future," Wathuti explained in a speech to the UN. "This is about making sure that the world right now is livable."[12]

The Kenyan government is also working to improve the country's environmental practices, preserve its habitats, and protect its people. Teen Kenyans are joining the fight to improve the environment both inside and outside the country. In 2017, after a study found that more than half of cows near cities had plastic bags in their stomachs, the country banned plastic carrier bags altogether. In addition, the country almost met its goal of 100 percent renewable energy. In 2021, 93 percent of the country's electricity came from renewable sources like hydropower or solar energy.[13] Activist Rahmina Paulette is working to combat pollution in Lake Victoria, and Eric Njuguna speaks at international conferences on climate change. A 2018 study found that most young Kenyans were hopeful that their lives would be better in the future. Today's young Kenyans are helping to make that future possible.

OFFICIAL NAME: REPUBLIC OF KENYA/ JAMHURI YA KENYA

GEOGRAPHY

Area: 224,081 square miles (580,367 sq km)

Highest Elevation: Mount Kenya at 17,057 feet (5,199 m)

Lowest Elevation: Indian Ocean at 0 feet (0 m)

PEOPLE

Population: 55.8 million (2022 est.)

Most Populous City: Nairobi (5.1 million)

Ethnic Groups: Kikuyu, Luhya, Kalenjin, Luo, others

Religions: Christianity, Islam

GOVERNMENT

Type of Government: Presidential republic

Capital: Nairobi

Head of State and Government: President

Legislature: Bicameral, with a Senate and National Assembly

ECONOMY

Currency: Kenyan shilling

Major Industries: Agriculture, small-scale goods, manufacturing, tourism

Natural Resources: Farmland, wildlife, limestones, soda ash, salt

NATIONAL SYMBOLS

National Animal: East African lion

National Anthem: "Ee Mungu Nguvu Yetu" ("Oh God of All Creation")

National Bird: Lilac-breasted roller

GLOSSARY

ALKALINE
An alkaline substance has pH levels higher than 7. A substance with a pH level lower than 7 is considered an acid.

BIOMETRIC
Relating to the use of body measurements to identify someone.

CAPITALIST
Having to do with an economic system where businesses are privately owned and operated in order to make a profit.

COLONIZATION
The practice of gaining political control over another country, occupying it with settlers, and exploiting its resources.

DEMARCATE
To clearly draw a line between or distinguish between things.

GROSS DOMESTIC PRODUCT (GDP)
The monetary value of all final goods and services produced within a nation's geographic borders over a specified period of time.

HYDROPOWER

Power generated from the movement of water.

MARITIME

Having to do with the sea or waterways.

MICROENTERPRISE

An extremely small business, sometimes owned and operated by just one person.

NOMADIC

Moving from one place to another.

PASTORALIST

People who live nomadic lifestyles and travel with their livestock herds.

POACHING

The illegal taking of wild animals.

TECTONIC PLATE

A huge piece of rock that makes up Earth's crust and upper mantle.

ADDITIONAL RESOURCES

SELECTED BIBLIOGRAPHY

Bain, Keith, et al. *Frommer's Kenya and Tanzania*. Wiley, 2010.

Elkins, Caroline. *Imperial Reckoning: The Untold Story of Britain's Gulag in Kenya*. Henry Holt and Company, 2005.

Rutherford, Adam. *A Brief History of Everyone Who Ever Lived: The Stories in Our Genes*. Weidenfeld & Nicolson, 2017.

FURTHER READINGS

Ham, Anthony, et al. *East Africa*. Lonely Planet, 2018.

Harris, Duchess, and Marcia Amidon Lusted. *The Transatlantic Slave Trade*. Abdo, 2020.

Kanogo, Tabitha. *Wangari Maathai*. Ohio University Press, 2020.

ONLINE RESOURCES

To learn more about Kenya, please visit **abdobooklinks.com** or scan this QR code. These links are routinely monitored and updated to provide the most current information available.

MORE INFORMATION

For more information on this subject, contact or visit the following organizations:

The Kenyan Embassy
2249 R St. NW
Washington, DC 20008
kenyaembassydc.org
The Kenyan Embassy represents the government and people of Kenya in the United States. It provides information about traveling to or living in Kenya.

The World Bank
Delta Center
Menengai Rd., Upper Hill
PO Box 30577-00100
Nairobi, Kenya
worldbank.org/en/country/kenya
The World Bank provides research and support for development and economic projects in Kenya.

The World Wildlife Fund
Property no.118,
Along Dagoretti Road, Karen
PO Box 62440-00200
Nairobi, Kenya
wwfkenya.org
The World Wildlife Fund works for the welfare of Kenyan wildlife and provides information about the country's biodiversity.

SOURCE NOTES

CHAPTER 1. A TOUR OF KENYA

1 "Weird Waters." *National Geographic*, n.d., education.nationalgeographic.org. Accessed 29 June 2022.

2. "Weird Waters," *National Geographic*.

3. "Kenya Population 2022." *World Population Review*, n.d., worldpopulationreview.com. Accessed 29 June 2022.

CHAPTER 2. GEOGRAPHY

1. "Kenya Population 2022." *World Population Review*, n.d., worldpopulationreview.com. Accessed 29 June 2022.

2. "Kenya Geography." *CountryReports*, n.d., countryreports.org. Accessed 29 June 2022.

3. "Geographical Overview of Kenya." *Embassy of the Republic of Kenya in Stockholm*, n.d., kenyaembassystockholm.com. Accessed 29 June 2022.

4. "Lamu." *Encyclopedia Britannica*, 8 Feb. 2018, britannica.com. Accessed 29 June 2022.

5. Mwenda Ntarangwi, et al. "Kenya." *Encyclopedia Britannica*, n.d., britannica.com. Accessed 29 June 2022.

6. Ntarangwi, et al., "Kenya," *Encyclopedia Britannica*.

7. "Kenya: Current Climate." *Climate Change Knowledge Portal*, n.d., climateknowledgeportal.worldbank.org. Accessed 29 June 2022.

8. "Kenya: Current Climate," *Climate Change Knowledge Portal*.

9. "UN Humanitarian Official Urges Attention to Drought in Kenya." *ABC News*, 13 May 2022, abcnews.go.com. Accessed 29 June 2022.

10. Carey Baraka. "A Drowning World: Kenya's Quiet Slide Underwater." *Guardian*, 17 Mar. 2022, theguardian.com. Accessed 29 June 2022.

CHAPTER 3. PLANTS AND ANIMALS

1. Richard Estes. "Gnu." *Encyclopedia Britannica*, 5 Mar. 2020, britannica.com. Accessed 5 July 2022.

2. "Big Cats." *Mara Conservancy*, n.d., maratriangle.org. Accessed 5 July 2022.

3. Jeheskel Shoshani. "Elephant." *Encyclopedia Britannica*, 29 Oct. 2021, britannica.com. Accessed 5 July 2022.

4. Lori Herbison Frame and George W. Frame. "Giraffe." *Encyclopedia Britannica*, 2 Sept. 2021, britannica.com. Accessed 5 July 2022.

5. "Kenya's Giraffe Conservation Guide." *Giraffe Conservation Foundation*, n.d., giraffeconservation.org. Accessed 5 July 2022.

6. "Rhinos." *Lewa Wildlife Conservancy*, n.d., lewa.org. Accessed 5 July 2022.

7. "Coastal and Marine Ecosystems of East Africa." *Kaskazi Environmental Alliance*, n.d., keainc.org. Accessed 5 July 2022.

8. Benjamin Cowburn, Robert D. Sluka, and Joy Smith. "Coral Reef Ecology and Biodiversity in Watamu Marine National Park, Kenya." *A Rocha Kenya*, Jan. 2013, arocha.or.ke. Accessed 5 July 2022.

9. "Coastal Kenya Programme." *WWF*, n.d., wwfkenya.org. Accessed 5 July 2022.

10. Anouk Zijlma. "Birds of Kenya, Africa." *TripSavvy*, 26 June 2019, tripsavvy.com. Accessed 5 July 2022.

11. "Kenya." *BirdLife International*, n.d., datazone.birdlife.org. Accessed 5 July 2022.

12. "Ostrich." *Encyclopedia Britannica*, 8 Apr. 2020, britannica.com. Accessed 5 July 2022.

13. "Arabuko Sokoke Forest Reserve." *African Horizons*, n.d., african-horizons.com. Accessed 5 July 2022.

14. "Tree Planting and Water Harvesting." *Green Belt Movement*, n.d., greenbeltmovement.org. Accessed 5 July 2022.

15. "Wangari Maathai." *Encyclopedia Britannica*, n.d., britannica.com. Accessed 11 Aug. 2022.

16. "The Giving Trees." *Sacramento News & Review*, 30 Dec. 2004, newsreview.com. Accessed 6 July 2022.

CHAPTER 4. HISTORY

1. Asher Omondi. "List of Most Spoken Languages in Kenya Apart from English and Kiswahili." *TUKO*, 30 Nov. 2021, tuko.co.ke. Accessed 5 July 2022.

2. Mark Cartwright. "Bantu Migration." *World History Encyclopedia*, 11 Apr. 2019, worldhistory.org. Accessed 5 July 2022.

3. "Mau Mau." *Encyclopedia Britannica*, 20 Mar. 2019, britannica.com. Accessed 5 July 2022.

4. Gregory Warner. "Britain Apologizes for Colonial-Era Torture of Kenyan Rebels." *NPR*, 9 June 2013, npr.org. Accessed 20 July 2022.

5. Jennifer Cooke. "Background on the Post-Election Crisis in Kenya." *CSIS*, 6 Aug. 2009, csis.org. Accessed 5 July 2022.

6. Kimiko de Freytas-Tamura. "President Uhuru Kenyatta Is Declared Victor of Kenyan Election." *New York Times*, 11 Aug. 2017, nytimes.com. Accessed 20 July 2022.

7. Amy McKenna. "Uhuru Kenyatta." *Encyclopedia Britannica*, 22 Oct. 2021, britannica.com. Accessed 5 July 2022.

SOURCE NOTES CONTINUED

CHAPTER 5. PEOPLE AND CULTURE

1. Asher Omondi. "List of Most Spoken Languages in Kenya Apart from English and Kiswahili." *TUKO*, 30 Nov. 2021, tuko.co.ke. Accessed 5 July 2022.

2. "Kenya—Ethnic Groups." *University of Pennsylvania: African Studies Center*, n.d., africa.upenn.edu. Accessed 5 July 2022.

3. "Luhya Tribe of Kenya." *Medium*, 5 Sept. 2020, medium.com. Accessed 5 July 2022.

4. "Kenya Population 2022." *World Population Review*, n.d., worldpopulationreview.com. Accessed 5 July 2022.

5. Jacob Poushter and Janell Fetterolf. "How People around the World View Religion's Role in Their Countries." *Pew Research Center*, 22 Apr. 2019, pewresearch.org. Accessed 5 July 2022.

6. "Kenya." *CIA World Factbook*, 21 June 2022, cia.gov. Accessed 5 July 2022.

7. Wycliffe W. Njororai Simiyu. "How Tokyo 2020 Tested Kenya's Running Dominance and Revealed Future Threats." *The Conversation*, 29 Aug. 2021, theconversation.com. Accessed 5 July 2022.

8. Bob Ramsak. "Kipchoge Breaks Two-Hour Barrier in Vienna." *World Athletics*, 12 Oct. 2019, worldathletics.org. Accessed 5 July 2022.

9. Emmanuel Onyango. "Why Kenyan Music Is Drowned Out by Nigerian Sounds." *BBC*, 23 Feb. 2022, bbc.com. Accessed 5 July 2022.

10. Onyango, "Why Kenyan Music Is Drowned Out by Nigerian Sounds," *BBC*.

11. "Binyavanga Wainaina Tells Us 'How to Write about Africa.'" *NPR*, 22 May 2019, npr.org. Accessed 13 July 2022.

CHAPTER 6. POLITICS

1. "Nairobi." *City Population*, n.d., citypopulation.de. Accessed 5 July 2022.

2. "About Us." *Mombasa County Government*, n.d., eservices.mombasa.go.ke. Accessed 5 July 2022.

3. "Kenya." *Freedom House*, n.d., freedomhouse.org. Accessed 20 July 2022.

4. Abdi Latif Dahir. "Kenya's Supreme Court Rejects President's Plan to Amend Constitution." *New York Times*, 31 Mar. 2022, nytimes.com. Accessed 5 July 2022.

5. "Kenya." *CIA World Factbook*, 21 June 2022, cia.gov. Accessed 5 July 2022.

6. "Kenya Attack: 147 Dead in Garissa University Assault." *BBC*, 3 Apr. 2015, bbc.com. Accessed 5 July 2022.

7. "Several People Killed in Suspected Al Shabaab Attack in Kenya." *France24*, 1 Mar. 2022, france24.com. Accessed 5 July 2022.

8. "Gov't Develops Comprehensive Maritime Security Strategy." *Kenya News Agency*, 8 Mar. 2022, kenyanews.go.ke. Accessed 5 July 2022.

CHAPTER 7. ECONOMICS

1. "Kenya." *CIA World Factbook*, 21 June 2022, cia.gov. Accessed 5 July 2022.

2. "Kenya Economic Update." *World Bank*, 9 June 2022, worldbank.org. Accessed 5 July 2022.

3. "Kenya," *CIA World Factbook*.

4. Douglas Kiereini. "Pyrethrum's Rich History in Kenya and Old Good Days." *Business Daily*, 3 Oct. 2019, businessdailyafrica.com. Accessed 5 July 2022.

5. "Cut Flowers in Kenya." *OEC*, n.d., oec.world. Accessed 5 July 2022.

6. Anuj Tanna. "Investing in Kenya's Young Micro-Entrepreneurs." *Project Syndicate*, 19 Mar. 2021, project-syndicate.org. Accessed 5 July 2022.

7. Julia Faria. "Share of Employment in Travel and Tourism in Kenya 2015–2020." *Statista*, 10 Aug. 2021, statista.com. Accessed 5 July 2022.

8. Wacera Ngunjiri. "Reviving Kenya's Tourism Industry after the COVID-19 Crisis." *DW*, 9 Mar. 2022, dw.com. Accessed 5 July 2022.

9. Rasna Warah. "'We Are on Our Knees': COVID's Impact on Kenya's Tourism." *ONE*, 12 Aug. 2021, one.org. Accessed 5 July 2022.

10. "Kenya," *CIA World Factbook*.

11. Susan Nyawira. "Kenya's Diaspora Remittances Hit Record High of Sh39.7bn in December." *allAfrica*, 16 Jan. 2022, allafrica.com. Accessed 5 July 2022.

12. Otiato Opali. "Chinese Companies Giving Back in Kenya." *China Daily*, 17 Dec. 2021, global.chinadaily.com.cn. Accessed 5 July 2022.

CHAPTER 8. KENYA TODAY

1. Aaron O'Neill. "Urbanization in Kenya 2020." *Statista*, 19 Jan. 2022, statista.com. Accessed 5 July 2022.

2. Constant Monda. "Survey: Nairobi Tycoons Now Control 86 Percent of City's Wealth." *Nairobi News*, 27 Mar. 2018, nairobinews.nation.africa. Accessed 5 July 2022.

3. "Kenya: Extreme Inequality in Numbers." *Oxfam International*, n.d., oxfam.org. Accessed 5 July 2022.

4. "Kenya." *CIA World Factbook*, 21 June 2022, cia.gov. Accessed 5 July 2022.

5. Abdi Latif Dahir. "Kenya Will Impose Widespread Restrictions on the Unvaccinated Starting Next Month." *New York Times*, 23 Nov. 2021, nytimes.com. Accessed 5 July 2022.

6. "Kenya Situation." *World Health Organization*, 13 July 2022, covid19.who.int. Accessed 13 July 2022.

7. "Kenyan Culture." *Cultural Atlas*, n.d., culturalatlas.sbs.com. Accessed 5 July 2022.

8. "New Drive Launched to Get 250,000 Out-of-School Children Back to Class in 16 Counties." *UNICEF*, 19 Oct. 2021, unicef.org. Accessed 5 July 2022.

9. "LGBT Rights in Kenya." *Equaldex*, n.d., equaldex.com. Accessed 5 July 2022.

10. "New Drive Launched," *UNICEF*.

11. "Kenya Dismisses Challenge to Its Ban on Female Genital Mutilation." *Reuters*, 17 Mar. 2021, reuters.com. Accessed 5 July 2022.

12. "Elizabeth Wathuti: We Can Change So Much in the World." *United Nations*, n.d., un.org. Accessed 20 July 2022.

13. Shadrack Kavilu. "Land Conflicts Are Slowing Kenya's Transition to Clean Energy." *Energy Monitor*, 5 Nov. 2021, energymonitor.ai. Accessed 5 July 2022.

ABOUT THE **AUTHOR**

A. W. BUCKEY

A. W. Buckey is a writer living in Brooklyn, New York. She has wanted to visit Mombasa ever since reading *The Travels of Ibn Battuta*.